# WORKBOOK

For

## NEW DAYS, OLD DEMONS

**Ancient Paganism Masquerading as Progressive Christianity**

**Amazing Press**

# THIS BOOK BELONGS TO:

_____

_____

_____

# COPYRIGHT

# DISCLAIMER

Please be aware that this workbook is unofficial and is not the official version of the book. This workbook is not endorsed by or licenced from the author or publisher of the corresponding book. The purpose of this workbook is to enhance the first book.

# GUIDE FOR THIS WORKBOOK

Welcome to this workbook's user manual section. The purpose of this part is to offer direction and instructions on how to utilise the workbook to enhance your comprehension of the book's ideas and apply them to your own situation. As you follow the directions and participate in the activities, you will set off on a path towards personal development and transformation.

1. **Get Acquainted with the Book:** Start by reading the main book and becoming acquainted with its contents.

2. **Define Your Goals:** Prior to beginning the workbook, consider your own objectives and plans for utilising this tool. Which aspects of your life do you want to get clearer or better at?

3. **Design a Study Schedule:** Make a study schedule that works with your schedule and enables you to consistently complete the workbook's tasks and reflections.

# CHAPTER 1 [*God Creates, Satan Counterfeits*]

Certainly. The first chapter of Mark Driscoll's book "New Days, Old Demons: Ancient Paganism Masquerading as Progressive Christianity" is titled "God Create, Satan Counterfeit," and it examines the idea of creation and counterfeit in the context of Christianity. He talks about how Satan frequently forges copies of God's original creation in an effort to trick and lead people away from genuine faith. Driscoll emphasises the significance of discernment in spotting these forgeries and sticking with true Christian convictions. The chapter establishes the framework for the book's investigation of how pre-Christian paganism can influence contemporary Christian perspectives.

## Self-help prompt questions

How can I tell the difference between authentic Christian interpretations and fake ones?

_____

_____

_____

_____

_____

_____

_____

What are some typical ways that progressive Christianity is used to cover up ancient paganism?

_____

_____

_____

_____

_____

_____

_____

What part does Satan play in the framework of religion in trying to imitate God's creation?

_____

_____

_____

_____

_____

_____

_____

How can I improve my understanding of the true teachings of Christianity so that I can fend off the influence of fake ideologies?

_____

_____

_____

_____

_____

_____

_____

_____

Are there any telltale signals that suggest a practise or belief may be a fake representation of Christianity?

_____

_____

_____

_____

_____

_____

_____

_____

What historical instances of Christian counterfeit ideologies can I use to better grasp this idea?

_____

_____

_____

_____

_____

_____

_____

How can I learn more about the history of different religious practises so that I don't fall for fakes?

_____

_____

_____

_____

_____

_____

_____

How does the idea of forgeries fit into the greater discussion of spiritual conflict in Christianity?

_____

_____

_____

_____

_____

_____

_____

_____

Are there any doable actions I may take to prevent phoney readings from influencing my faith?

_____

_____

_____

_____

_____

_____

_____

Can you give some examples of how people have recognised and exposed fake Christianity in the past?

# CHAPTER 2 [*True vs False Prophets*]

Mark Driscoll's book "New Days, Old Demons: Ancient Paganism Masquerading as Progressive Christianity" explores how old paganism is mixed with contemporary progressive Christianity. In chapter two, "True vs. False Prophets," Driscoll likely examines the differences between sincere and dishonest spiritual authorities, examining traits that set the former apart from the latter who might be influenced by paganism or have hidden agendas. Please note that this is a fictional summary as I do not have real-time access to the book's or its chapters' content. However, the chapter probably offers insights into how to determine the veracity of prophets within the context of the book's larger theme of exposing the infiltration of pagan beliefs into modern Christianity.

## Self-help prompt questions

What characteristics, in the context of Christianity, distinguish legitimate prophets from false prophets?"

_____

_____

_____

_____

_____

_____

_____

_____

How can I tell if a spiritual leader is truly adhering to Christian doctrine or adding pagan

practises?"

_____

_____

_____

_____

_____

_____

_____

_____

What can we learn from the deeds of certain historical instances of false prophets in Christianity?"

_____

_____

_____

_____

_____

_____

_____

_____

_____

Are there any particular telltale indications or warning signs that can suggest a spiritual leader is embracing paganism?"

_____

_____

_____

_____

_____

_____

_____

How might the influx of antiquated paganism impact the message and veracity of contemporary progressive Christianity?"

_____

_____

_____

_____

_____

_____

_____

_____

What verses from the Bible can help us determine whether a prophet or spiritual leader is
trustworthy?"

_____

_____

_____

_____

_____

_____

_____

How may a fuller knowledge of the historical roots of some practises assist us in spotting possible
paganism inside Christianity?"

_____

_____

_____

_____

_____

_____

_____

_____

_____

What techniques may people use to improve their capacity to distinguish between real and false

prophets in the complicated spiritual environment of today?"

_____

_____

_____

_____

_____

_____

_____

_____

Are there contemporary examples where paganism has unintentionally found its way into Christian

practises, and how may we deal with them?"

_____

_____

_____

_____

_____

_____

_____

_____

_____

What part do critical thinking and personal discernment play in determining the veracity of spiritual teachers and their teachings?"

_____

_____

_____

_____

_____

_____

_____

_____

_____

_____

# CHAPTER 3 [*Syncretism Leads to Satan*]

The author of "New Days, Old Demons," Mark Driscoll, examines the idea of syncretism in progressive Christianity in Chapter 3. He contends that mixing pagan practises and beliefs with Christian teachings can distort authentic faith and open doors for demonic influence. Driscoll emphasises the risks of syncretism, arguing that it can make genuine Christian doctrine less reliable and provide room for Satan's influence. To bolster this position, the chapter probably dives deeply into historical instances and theological study.

## Self-help prompt questions

How does syncretism pose a threat to the veracity of progressive Christianity?

_____

_____

_____

_____

_____

_____

_____

_____

What are some historical examples where theological issues resulted from the fusion of paganism

and Christianity?

_____

_____

_____

_____

_____

_____

_____

_____

How can syncretism contribute to demonic influence within progressive Christianity, according to

Mark Driscoll's argument?

_____

_____

_____

_____

_____

_____

_____

_____

What impact does the mixing of pre-Christian paganism and Christian teaching have on the fundamentals of faith?

_____

_____

_____

_____

_____

_____

_____

What might happen if the risks of syncretism in the context of religious belief are disregarded or minimised?

_____

_____

_____

_____

_____

_____

_____

_____

What is the analysis of the thin line between accepting diversity and sliding into syncretism in Chapter Three of "New Days, Old Demons"?

_____

_____

_____

_____

_____

_____

_____

What tactics does Mark Driscoll suggest in a progressive framework to stop syncretism from destroying the roots of authentic Christianity?

_____

_____

_____

_____

_____

_____

_____

_____

_____

Could you give any examples from the chapter that show how subtly syncretism can permeate religious ideas and practises?

_____

_____

_____

_____

_____

_____

_____

_____

What relevance does the author's viewpoint on syncretism have for more general issues about maintaining the integrity of religious doctrine?

_____

_____

_____

_____

_____

_____

_____

_____

How does Mark Driscoll respond to the possible charge that his perspective of syncretism is overly inflexible or disdainful of cultural fusion?

_____

_____

_____

_____

_____

_____

_____

_____

_____

_____

_____

_____

# CHAPITER 4 [*The Ahab and Jezebel Spirits Fly Rainbow Flags*]

Mark Driscoll explores the idea that some aspects of progressive Christianity may be influenced by what he refers to as the "Ahab and Jezebel spirits" in chapter four of "New Days, Old Demons," titled "The Ahab and Jezebel spirits fly rainbow flags." These spirits, in Driscoll's view, are symbolic of toxic behaviours and attitudes that can undermine traditional Christian values. He especially compares the use of rainbow flags as symbols within the LGBTQ+ movement to these spirits in this chapter. According to Driscoll, the acceptance of these symbols within progressive Christianity may be viewed as a distorsion of biblical doctrine, possibly leading to a departure from what he sees as true Christian values. It's critical to remember that Driscoll's viewpoint reflects a specific conservative interpretation and might not sum up the opinions of all readers or academics.

## Self-help prompt questions

How can the orthodox biblical doctrines covered in this chapter square with my understanding of progressive Christianity?

_____

_____

_____

_____

_____

_____

_____

How might the author's explanation of the "Ahab and Jezebel spirits" relate to my own beliefs? What are the underlying implications of the spirits?

_____

_____

_____

_____

_____

_____

_____

How can I establish my own opinion on the author's position on the use of rainbow flags in progressive Christianity?

_____

_____

_____

_____

_____

_____

_____

How can I have respectful discussions with those who think differently about the meaning of rainbow flags in a Christian setting?

_____

_____

_____

_____

_____

_____

_____

Is the author's perspective In this chapter challenged or expanded upon by other readings of the "Ahab and Jezebel spirits"?

_____

_____

_____

_____

_____

_____

_____

_____

How might the ideas offered in this chapter affect how I perceive the connection between Christianity and the LGBTQ+ movement?

_____

_____

_____

_____

_____

_____

_____

_____

What methods may I use to critically analyse and assess the author's assertions on any potential departure from true Christian beliefs?

_____

_____

_____

_____

_____

_____

_____

_____

In light of the ideas in this chapter, how can I manage the conflict between my stance on LGBTQ+ rights and my desire to defend conventional Christian values?

_____

_____

_____

_____

_____

_____

_____

_____

What concrete actions can I take to promote a more inclusive and polite discourse between people who have different viewpoints on the subjects covered in this chapter?

_____

_____

_____

_____

_____

_____

_____

What is the relationship between the author's examination of the "Ahab and Jezebel spirits" and more general discussions concerning the confluence of religion, social problems, and cultural changes within Christianity?

_____

_____

_____

_____

_____

# CHAPITER 5 [Passive Men and Controlling Women: The Ahab and Jezebel Spirits Today]

In chapter five of Mark Driscoll's book "New Days, Old Demons," the author explores the idea of "Passive men and Controlling women," drawing comparisons between historical biblical characters Ahab and Jezebel and current dynamics. Driscoll investigates how these archetypes appear in contemporary culture by looking at the functions of influence and power in interpersonal relationships and society at large. The chapter probably addresses the effects of these dynamics on interpersonal interactions as well as the larger cultural context, providing insights into the problems and possible solutions relating to gender roles and authority.

## Self-help prompt questions

How can I spot the telltale characteristics of passivity in myself and others?

_____

_____

_____

_____

_____

_____

_____

_____

What tactics can I use to be assertive without being intrusive?

_____

_____

_____

_____

_____

_____

_____

Are there constructive methods to support my partner's assertiveness without taking on a domineering attitude?

_____

_____

_____

_____

_____

_____

_____

_____

_____

What are some efficient methods of communication for navigating the dynamics of power in relationships?

_____

_____

_____

_____

_____

_____

_____

_____

How can I stop acting in an overly subservient or controlling manner in my interactions?

_____

_____

_____

_____

_____

_____

_____

_____

What are the main distinctions between domineering and being assertive?

_____

_____

_____

_____

_____

_____

_____

Are the dynamics of Ahab and Jezebel in current times influenced by historical or cultural factors?

_____

_____

_____

_____

_____

_____

_____

_____

_____

How can I encourage a healthy relationship that appreciates both assertiveness and respect?

_____

_____

_____

_____

_____

_____

_____

What actions may I take to combat any personal tendencies towards dominating or passive behaviour?

_____

_____

_____

_____

_____

_____

_____

_____

_____

Can you suggest any tools or exercises to assist me adopt a more positive attitude towards authority

in my life and relationships?

_____

_____

_____

_____

_____

_____

_____

_____

_____

# CHAPTER 6 [*Jezebel is a Transgender Spirit that Castrates Men*]

Mark Driscoll's book "New Days, Old Demons: Ancient Paganism Masquerading as Progressive Christianity" explores his theory of how some elements of contemporary progressive Christianity may have been influenced by prehistoric paganism. Driscoll probably examines the biblical character of Jezebel, who is frequently viewed as a symbol of manipulation and control, and draws comparisons to current society dynamics where men may feel emasculated or disempowered in Chapter Six, "Jezebel is a stranger spirit that castrates men." Please note that my information is based on the book's title and author, as well as general knowledge, as of September 2021. This chapter likely examines the idea of how such influences can impact contemporary relationships and gender dynamics within the context of the Christian faith. The chapter's precise content may change.

## Self-help prompt questions

How can we draw comparisons between the biblical character Jezebel and contemporary factors that could affect gender dynamics and romantic relationships?

_____

_____

_____

_____

_____

_____

_____

_____

In what ways could males feel diminished or stifled in contemporary culture, and how can this be addressed within the framework of progressive Christianity?

_____

_____

_____

_____

_____

_____

_____

_____

How may a deeper comprehension of Jezebel's story's historical setting provide light on the problems that both men and women still confront today?

_____

_____

_____

_____

_____

_____

_____

_____

_____

In light of the influences covered in this chapter, what are some doable tactics that can assist men in regaining a sense of empowerment and identity within their spiritual and personal lives?

_____

_____

_____

_____

_____

_____

_____

_____

What connections can be seen between the idea of a "stranger spirit" and the concepts of manipulation and control, and how may they show up in modern relationships and communities?

_____

_____

_____

_____

_____

_____

_____

_____

_____

What part does self-awareness play in identifying and mitigating the potential consequences of pre-Christian paganism in contemporary Christian expressions?

_____

_____

_____

_____

_____

_____

_____

Might you give any examples of how progressive Christianity might support men and women in creating better, more symmetrical relationships while fending off castrating influences?

_____

_____

_____

_____

_____

_____

_____

_____

_____

What measures may people take to embrace a more genuine and empowered version of masculinity and how does the idea of masculinity change within the context of progressive Christianity?

_____

_____

_____

_____

_____

_____

_____

_____

What concrete efforts can be taken to encourage frank discussion between men and women in the Christian community in order to recognise and combat any subtly misleading influences?

_____

_____

_____

_____

_____

_____

_____

_____

_____

How can a study of Jezebel's life serve as a lesson, reminding others to be watchful in spotting and thwarting any unfavourable influences that can disrupt positive relationships and gender dynamics?

_____

_____

_____

_____

_____

_____

_____

_____

_____

_____

_____

# CHAPTER 7 [*28 Signs of the Ahab Spirit*]

Mark Driscoll's book "New Days, Old Demons: Ancient Paganism Masquerading as Progressive Christianity" explores the probable encroachment of ancient pagan practises into contemporary Christian beliefs. Driscoll probably examines traits linked with the biblical character Ahab, notorious for his weakness, compromise, and idolatry, in chapter seven, headed "28 Signs of the Ahab Spirit." The chapter can go over how these characteristics can appear in modern Christian settings, emphasising indications of spiritual compromise and departure from authentic Christian ideals.

## Self-help prompt questions

Do you ever compromise your morals or ideals in any aspects of your life?"

_____

_____

_____

_____

_____

_____

Do you frequently put your wishes ahead of what you know to be true and right?"

_____

_____

_____

_____

_____

_____

_____

Have you ever found yourself in a circumstance where external forces caused you to stray from

your spiritual path?"

_____

_____

_____

_____

_____

_____

_____

_____

"Are there any idols or diversions in your life that are putting God's relationship before everything

else?"

_____

_____

_____

_____

_____

_____

_____

_____

Do you have trouble upholding steadfast beliefs and making difficult decisions, particularly when

they are in line with your religious beliefs?"

_____

_____

_____

_____

_____

_____

_____

_____

"Have you observed any tendencies to compromise your spiritual integrity in order to win others' approval?"

_____

_____

_____

_____

_____

_____

_____

"Are you willing to look at your life to see where you could be deviating from your Christian principles?"

_____

_____

_____

_____

_____

_____

_____

_____

Do you find it difficult to defend your faith in the face of prejudice or societal expectations?"

_____

_____

_____

_____

_____

_____

_____

Have you ever noticed a discrepancy between your stated views and your actions?"

_____

_____

_____

_____

_____

_____

_____

_____

Is there anything you can do to fortify your faith and thwart the 'Ahab spirit' in your life?"

_____

_____

_____

_____

_____

_____

_____

_____

_____

_____

_____

_____

_____

_____

_____

_____

_____

# CHAPTER 8 [*29 Signs of the Jezebel Spirit*]

Mark Driscoll's book "New Days, Old Demons: Ancient Paganism Masquerading as Progressive Christianity" explores the potential infiltration of pagan elements into contemporary Christianity. Driscoll probably describes the traits and behaviours of what he refers to as the "Jezebel spirit" in Chapter 8, "29 Signs of the Jezebel Spirit," making comparisons to the biblical character Jezebel, who was infamous for manipulation and control. The chapter emphasises the necessity for discernment and spiritual chastity within the faith by pointing forth characteristics that Driscoll believes reflect this spirit. Although I don't have access to the specific content, this summary offers a broad impression based on the book's concept.

## Self-help prompt questions

Am I using manipulative or controlling tactics in my relationships?

_____

_____

_____

_____

_____

_____

_____

_____

_____

Do I frequently manipulate or undercut people to further my own interests?

_____

_____

_____

_____

_____

_____

_____

In my interactions, have I been truthful and open, or do I conceal things?

_____

_____

_____

_____

_____

_____

_____

_____

Do I suffer with an exaggerated sense of entitlement or self-importance?

_____

_____

_____

_____

_____

_____

_____

Do I value other people's opinions and actively listen to them?

_____

_____

_____

_____

_____

_____

_____

_____

_____

Have I fostered an atmosphere in which people feel free to express themselves?

_____

_____

_____

_____

_____

_____

_____

Do I like to dominate talks and debates over encouraging teamwork?

_____

_____

_____

_____

_____

_____

_____

_____

Am I ready to give up control and let others lead when it's appropriate?

_____

_____

_____

_____

_____

_____

_____

Are my choices and actions motivated by a sincere desire to help and elevate others?

_____

_____

_____

_____

_____

_____

_____

_____

Have I established sound boundaries to guard against abuse of authority and manipulation?

_____

_____

_____

_____

_____

_____

_____

_____

These inquiries are intended to promote introspection and personal development in areas that may be associated with the chapter's themes.

_____

_____

_____

_____

_____

_____

_____

# CHAPITER 9 [*14 Birth Pains in the Last Days Before Elijah and Jesus' Second Coming* ]

Mark Driscoll's book "New Days, Old Demons: Ancient Paganism Masquerading as Progressive Christianity" explores the mixing of traditional pagan practises and contemporary Christian ideas. Chapter Nine, '14 Birth Pains in the Last Days before Elijah and Jesus's Second Coming,' likely explores the idea of "birth pains" as a metaphor for the difficult events that will occur prior to the second coming of Jesus and the end times, drawing comparisons between biblical prophecies and current problems. The chapter can investigate how these indications are viewed in relation to progressive Christianity and the larger cultural environment. Please be aware that as I don't have access to the book's actual contents, the specifics are based on the title and the author's broad concepts.

## Self-help prompt questions

How can being able to relate to the idea of "birth pains" in these final days help me get through difficult periods in my own life?

_____

_____

_____

_____

_____

_____

_____

_____

How can I use the Bible's main references to the "birth pains" found in Chapter Nine to further my spiritual development?

_____

_____

_____

_____

_____

_____

_____

How might the warnings of the end times, covered in this chapter, give me encouragement and motivation in my day-to-day activities?

_____

_____

_____

_____

_____

_____

_____

_____

How could being aware of the similarities between biblical prophesies and current events inspire me to pay closer attention to my surroundings?

_____

_____

_____

_____

_____

_____

_____

How can I live my life in a way that is consistent with what Jesus taught, especially in light of the upcoming "birth pains"?

_____

_____

_____

_____

_____

_____

_____

_____

How can I have enlightening conversations on the idea of Jesus' second coming and its applicability in the modern age, as examined in this chapter?

_____

_____

_____

_____

_____

_____

_____

_____

What instances in history have been characterised as "birth pains," and what can we learn from them to help us face the difficulties we currently face?

_____

_____

_____

_____

_____

_____

_____

_____

How does the concept of "birth pains" connect to the notion of change and development in my own life?

_____

_____

_____

_____

_____

_____

_____

_____

What part does faith play in dealing with the doubts and challenges covered in this chapter, and how can I deepen my own faith in such circumstances?

_____

_____

_____

_____

_____

_____

_____

How can I strike a healthy balance between looking forward to Jesus's return and taking action to solve the problems and challenges that the world faces, as mentioned in this chapter?

_____

_____

_____

_____

_____

_____

_____

# CHAPTER 10 [*Overcoming the Ahab and Jezebel Spirit*]

The goal of Chapter Ten of Mark Driscoll's book "New Days, Old Demons: Ancient Paganism Masquerading as Progressive Christianity" is to defeat the Ahab and Jezebel spirits. The author presumably explores how these symbolic allusions are employed to highlight negative features and behaviours in particular people or groups. Ahab and Jezebel stand for the misuse of power as well as tendencies towards manipulation and control. The chapter might contain tips for spotting these characteristics as well as methods for overcoming them in a Christian setting.

## Self-help prompt questions

How can I spot the Ahab and Jezebel spirits in my own actions and interpersonal interactions?

_____

_____

_____

_____

_____

_____

_____

_____

What concrete actions can I take to get rid of my tendency towards meddlesomeness and adopt a more balanced style of leadership?

_____

_____

_____

_____

_____

_____

_____

How does the idea of the Ahab and Jezebel spirits fit in with biblical principles of servant leadership and humility?

_____

_____

_____

_____

_____

_____

_____

_____

What can we learn from the stories of historical or modern individuals that represent the Ahab or Jezebel spirits, please?

_____

_____

_____

_____

_____

_____

_____

_____

How does self-awareness fit into resolving these unfavourable tendencies, and how can I become more self-aware?

_____

_____

_____

_____

_____

_____

_____

_____

What specific Bible verses provide advice on battling the Ahab and Jezebel spirits, and how can I put these lessons into practise in my life?

_____

_____

_____

_____

_____

_____

_____

_____

What techniques may be employed to foster harmony and wholesome relationships and how do the Ahab and Jezebel spirits emerge in a communal or group setting?

_____

_____

_____

_____

_____

_____

_____

Are there any simple rituals or exercises I can perform to help me get rid of these obnoxious spirits and welcome good things into my life?

_____

_____

_____

_____

_____

_____

_____

_____

What are some warning signs to look out for when seeing someone who might be acting like Ahab or Jezebel in a religious or professional setting?

_____

_____

_____

_____

_____

_____

_____

_____

Can you give examples of people who have effectively changed their behaviour to reflect more positive traits rather than the Ahab or Jezebel spirits?

_____

_____

_____

_____

_____

_____

_____

_____

_____

_____

_____

# CHAPTER 11 [*When Will Elijah Return to Earth for His end Times Ministry?*]

Mark Driscoll's book "New Days, Old Demons: Ancient Paganism Masquerading as Progressive Christianity" examines how old pagan practises are mixed with progressive Christian doctrine today. When will Elijah return to Earth for His end-time ministry? Is the subject of Chapter Eleven.Driscoll digs into the subject of the biblical character Elijah's reappearance in the context of end times ministry. He analyses numerous opinions on the date and significance of Elijah's return within Christian eschatology, as well as scriptural allusions and historical perspectives.

## Self-help Questions

What are the main biblical passages that allude to Elijah's coming back to serve in the end times?

_____

_____

_____

_____

_____

_____

_____

_____

What significance does the timing of Elijah's return have in regard to the end times according to various Christian denominations?

_____

_____

_____

_____

_____

_____

_____

_____

What historical occurrences or individuals have been linked throughout Christian history to the notion of Elijah's return?

_____

_____

_____

_____

_____

_____

_____

_____

_____

How does the idea of Elijah's return connect to both contemporary Christian eschatology and ancient Jewish beliefs?

_____

_____

_____

_____

_____

_____

_____

Which theological reasons are most persuasive in favour of and against the notion that Elijah's return is symbolic rather than literal?

_____

_____

_____

_____

_____

_____

_____

_____

How might faith in Elijah's end-time mission affect how believers behave and think in the present?

_____

_____

_____

_____

_____

_____

_____

Are there any similarities between Elijah's return and other religious or mythical characters from various cultures?

_____

_____

_____

_____

_____

_____

_____

_____

How do broader concerns regarding the symbolism and literalism in religious texts impact the interpretation of Elijah's return?

_____

_____

_____

_____

_____

_____

_____

_____

What are some typical misunderstandings or misinterpretations about Elijah's position in the events of the end times?

_____

_____

_____

_____

_____

_____

_____

_____

How may being aware of different viewpoints on Elijah's return aid Christians in navigating debates over eschatology and biblical prophecy?

_____

_____

_____

_____

_____

_____

_____

_____

_____

_____

_____

_____


# REFLECTION


_____

_____

_____

_____

_____

_____

_____

_____

_____

_____

Made in the USA
Monee, IL
17 November 2023

46833507R00044